EARTHQUAKES

EARLY BIRD EARTH SCIENCE

BY SALLY M. WALKER

LERNER PUBLICATIONS COMPANY • MINNEAPOLIS

The images in this book are used with the permission of: Courtesy National Information Service for Earthquake Engineering, University of California, Berkeley, pp. 1, 4, 6 (background), 9 (background), 18 (background), 30 (background), 32, 36 (background), 44–45 (background), 46–47 (background); U.S. Geological Survey, pp. 1 (title type), 9, 26, 47; © Getty Images, pp. 5, 6, 8, 18, 22, 24, 28, 30, 31, 34, 35, 38, 48 (both); © Eda Rogers, p. 7; © Stephanie Konfal/USGS/Handout/Reuters/CORBIS, p. 10; © Altitude/Peter Arnold, Inc., p. 13; © Raymond Gehman/CORBIS, p. 14; © Brie Cohen/Independent Picture Service, p. 15; © Tom Bean/CORBIS, p. 17; © Bettmann/CORBIS, pp. 19, 27; PhotoDisc Royalty Free by Getty Images, p. 20; Courtesy of Idaho National Laboratory, p. 23; © John R. Kreul/Independent Picture Service, p. 25; © Reuters/CORBIS, p. 29; © Jessie Carbonaro/iStockphoto, p. 36, © Michael S. Yamashita/CORBIS, pp. 37, 46; © Sam Lund/Independent Picture Service, p. 39; © Adam Jones/Visuals Unlimited, p. 40; © Sean Sprague/Photo Agora, p. 41; © Roger Ressmeyer/CORBIS, p. 42; © Paul Nicklen/National Geographic/Getty Images, p. 43.

Front Cover: © Mark Downey/Lucid Images/CORBIS.
Front Cover Title Type: U.S. Geological Survey.
Back Cover: © Reuters/CORBIS.

Illustrations on pp. 11, 12, 16, 21, 33 by Laura Westlund, copyright © by Lerner Publishing Group, Inc.

Lerner Publications Company
A division of Lerner Publishing Group, Inc.
241 First Avenue North
Minneapolis, MN 55401 U.S.A.

Website address: www.lernerbooks.com

Library of Congress Cataloging-in-Publication Data

Walker, Sally M.
    Earthquakes / by Sally M. Walker.
       p.   cm. — (Early bird earth science)
    Includes index.
    ISBN-13: 978–0–8225–6735–6 (lib. bdg. : alk. paper)
    ISBN-10: 0–8225–6735–0 (lib. bdg. : alk. paper)
    1. Earthquakes—Juvenile literature.   I. Title.
QE521.3.W348 2008
551.22—dc22   2006027103

Manufactured in the United States of America
1 2 3 4 5 6 – JR – 13 12 11 10 09 08

CONTENTS

BE A WORD DETECTIVE

Can you find these words as you read about earthquakes? Be a detective and try to figure out what they mean. You can turn to the glossary on page 46 for help.

aftershock	forces	seismic waves
crust	magnitude	seismograph
energy	mantle	seismologists
fault	plates	tsunami
focus	Richter scale	vibrate

This pile of concrete used to be a building. The building fell down because the ground beneath it shook. What is it called when the ground shakes?

CHAPTER 1

WHAT IS AN EARTHQUAKE?

On October 8, 2005, children in the country of Pakistan sat in school. Suddenly the ground started to shake. Soil and rocks tumbled down hills onto roads. Many houses and some schools fell down. It was an earthquake!

Earthquakes happen because of forces inside Earth. Forces are pushes and pulls. Strong forces push and pull rock beneath Earth's surface. Rock seems very hard to us. But forces inside Earth are strong enough to twist and stretch it.

Over millions of years, forces have twisted the layers of this rock.

Stretching rock can make it break. When rock inside Earth breaks, the ground trembles. Shaking ground is called an earthquake. Strong earthquakes can cause a lot of damage.

This house broke apart when an earthquake shook it.

In 1989, a strong earthquake shook San Francisco. It made part of the Oakland Bay Bridge fall down. Where else can earthquakes happen?

CHAPTER 2

COULD EARTHQUAKES SHAKE YOUR TOWN?

Earthquakes begin in rock that is buried beneath Earth's surface. They can happen anywhere. But some places have more earthquakes than others.

These seismologists are setting up tools that measure ground movement.

Seismologists (size-MAH-luh-jists) are scientists who study earthquakes. These scientists have carefully studied Earth's surface. They think they know why earthquakes happen in some places more than others.

About 10 large slabs of rock cover Earth's surface. Slabs are thick, flat pieces. These rock slabs are called plates. They are much thicker than a dinner plate, though. Earth's plates are about 60 miles thick. They are thinner under oceans and thicker under mountains.

Earth's crust makes up the top part of each plate. The crust is the outside layer of Earth. Beneath the crust is the layer of Earth called the mantle. Part of the mantle forms the lower part of the plates.

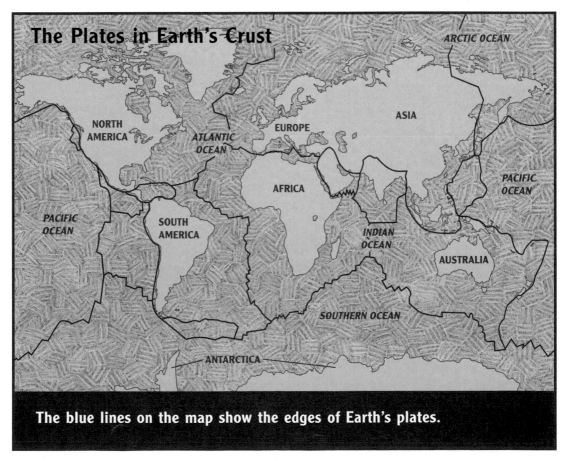

The Plates in Earth's Crust

ARCTIC OCEAN

ASIA

NORTH AMERICA

EUROPE

ATLANTIC OCEAN

AFRICA

PACIFIC OCEAN

PACIFIC OCEAN

SOUTH AMERICA

INDIAN OCEAN

AUSTRALIA

SOUTHERN OCEAN

ANTARCTICA

The blue lines on the map show the edges of Earth's plates.

The rock that makes up each plate is often brittle. Brittle rock cracks easily. Land and oceans sit on top of the brittle plates.

Another layer of rock lies beneath the plates, lower in Earth's mantle. This rock can bend and twist without breaking. It is called plastic rock. The brittle plates float on top of the plastic rock. The plates move slowly into new positions. A plate moves about as fast as your fingernail grows. That's only 1 or 2 inches a year.

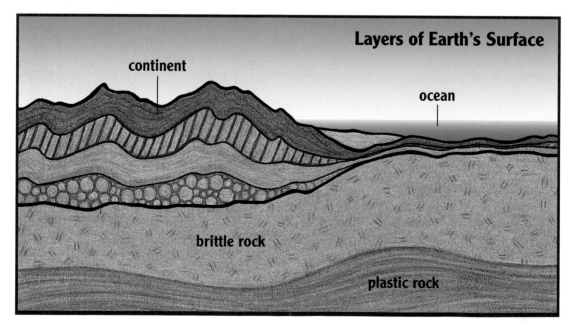

Layers of Earth's Surface

continent

ocean

brittle rock

plastic rock

The Great Rift Valley is in Africa. The valley formed as two of Earth's plates have slowly drifted apart.

Most earthquakes happen near the edges of the plates. Sometimes the brittle plates overlap one another as they float on the plastic rock. Some plates scrape against one another. Other plates drift farther apart.

When the plates move, pressure builds up in the brittle rock. Forces squeeze and stretch the rock. That changes the rock's shape. As it changes shape, the brittle rock cracks.

Over time, forces have created many cracks in this rock.

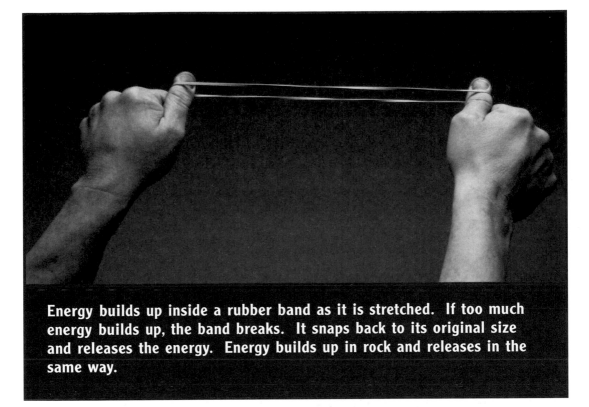

Energy builds up inside a rubber band as it is stretched. If too much energy builds up, the band breaks. It snaps back to its original size and releases the energy. Energy builds up in rock and releases in the same way.

Forces keep pushing and pulling at the rock on each side of a crack. Energy builds up inside the rock. Energy is the power to make something move.

Sometimes too much energy builds up. So the rock on one side of the crack jerks loose from the other side. Once the sides of a crack have moved, the crack is called a fault (FAWLT).

Most faults are slanted. Rock along a slanted fault moves up or down. Other faults are straight up and down. Rock along this kind of fault slips sideways.

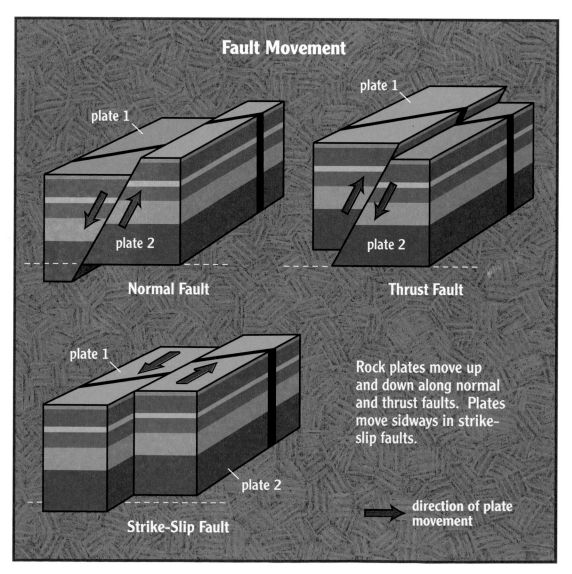

Fault Movement

plate 1

plate 2

Normal Fault

plate 1

plate 2

Thrust Fault

plate 1

plate 2

Strike-Slip Fault

Rock plates move up and down along normal and thrust faults. Plates move sidways in strike-slip faults.

→ direction of plate movement

Along the San Andreas Fault, you can see where two of Earth's plates meet. The fault is about 600 miles long.

One famous fault in California is called the San Andreas Fault. It is hundreds of miles long. Rock slips sideways along the San Andreas Fault. Many earthquakes happen along this fault.

A huge earthquake happened in Japan in 1995. The rock movement that caused the earthquake was not far below Earth's surface. Why is an earthquake's starting point important?

CHAPTER 3
WAVES INSIDE EARTH

The starting point of an earthquake is called the focus. It is the underground spot where the rock first breaks loose along a fault. The closer the focus is to the surface, the more damage the earthquake can cause.

Rock moves along a fault for only a minute or two. But people often feel the ground shake for several minutes. Seismic (SIZE-mihk) waves cause the ground to keep shaking after the rock stops moving. Seismic waves are waves of energy that move through Earth.

In 1964, an earthquake shook the city of Anchorage, Alaska. The shaking lasted four minutes. It caused a lot of damage.

Seismic waves can spread out through the ground, just like waves spread through water.

Imagine throwing a rock into a puddle. Waves of water spread out from the spot where the rock fell. Seismic waves spread out from the focus of an earthquake in a similar way. They spread through the ground. Their energy causes the ground to vibrate (VEYE-brate). Vibrating is a kind of shaking.

An earthquake causes all the tiny parts inside rock to vibrate. Some waves make the inside parts of rock push against other parts. Other waves make rock shake from side to side. And some waves make the inside parts of rock move in circles. Buildings and roads can fall apart when seismic waves shake rock from side to side or in circles.

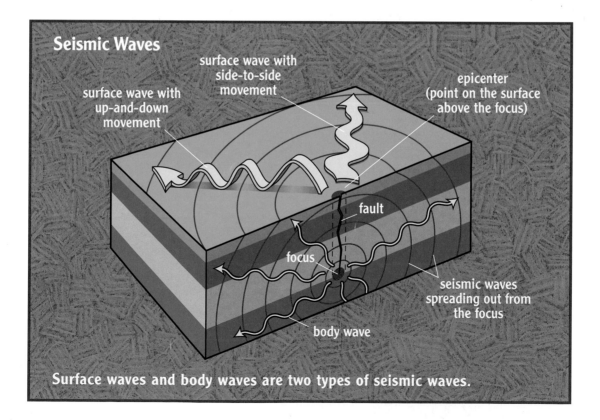

Seismic Waves

surface wave with side-to-side movement

surface wave with up-and-down movement

epicenter (point on the surface above the focus)

fault

focus

seismic waves spreading out from the focus

body wave

Surface waves and body waves are two types of seismic waves.

A seismograph (SIZE-muh-graf) is a scientific tool. It records which directions the ground moves during an earthquake. The ground could move up and down. It could also move north to south and east to west.

The machines on the left are seismographs. They recorded ground movement in a 2004 earthquake in the Philippines.

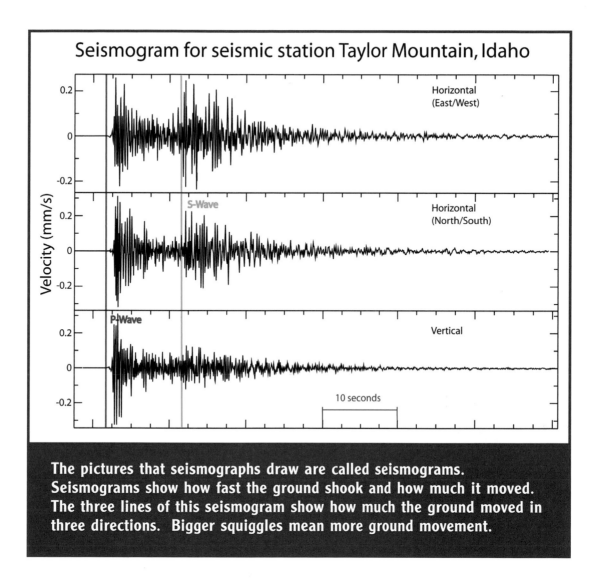

Seismogram for seismic station Taylor Mountain, Idaho

Horizontal (East/West)

S-Wave

Horizontal (North/South)

P-Wave

Vertical

Velocity (mm/s)

10 seconds

The pictures that seismographs draw are called seismograms. Seismograms show how fast the ground shook and how much it moved. The three lines of this seismogram show how much the ground moved in three directions. Bigger squiggles mean more ground movement.

Seismographs draw pictures to show how the ground moved. The pictures are made up of squiggly lines. Each line stands for one seismic wave.

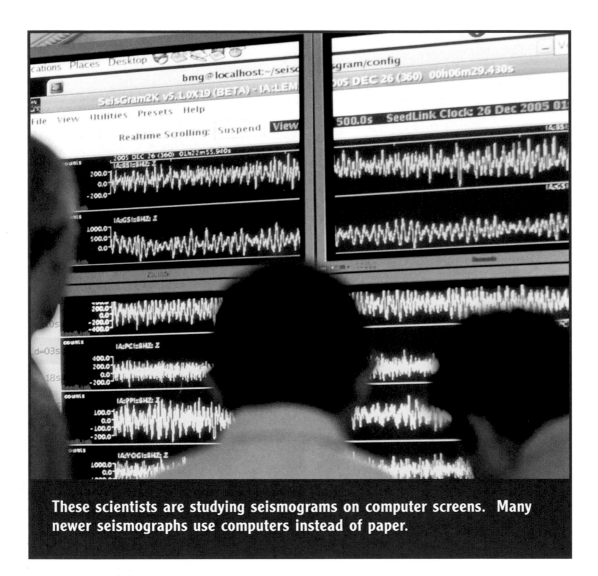

These scientists are studying seismograms on computer screens. Many newer seismographs use computers instead of paper.

Seismographs record how long an earthquake lasted. They also record how fast the seismic waves moved. Some waves travel more than 250 miles per hour. That's faster than a race car. Others move more slowly. They move about as fast as a car on the highway. Seismic waves can travel hundreds of miles. They get weaker and weaker as they move away from the focus.

Some seismic waves move faster through water than through the ground. Other seismic waves can't travel through liquid at all.

A seismograph's squiggly lines show how much the ground moved during an earthquake. Scientists study the lines to measure the earthquake's magnitude (MAG-nih-tood). Magnitude is the strength of an earthquake.

The earthquake in Alaska in 1964 was one of the strongest earthquakes ever. It ripped apart the two sides of this road.

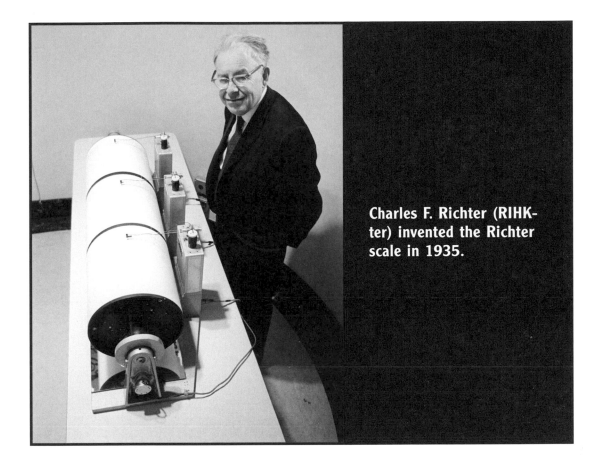

Charles F. Richter (RIHK-ter) invented the Richter scale in 1935.

The Richter scale is used to describe an earthquake's magnitude. The Richter scale is a number scale. Numbers 1 and 2 are for very weak earthquakes. Usually people don't even feel those quakes. But they do feel earthquakes that measure 5 or 6. So far, the strongest earthquake ever was a little more than 9 on the Richter scale.

The strongest earthquake ever recorded happened in Chile in 1960.

Hundreds of thousands of small quakes happen each year. People can hardly feel them. Very strong earthquakes are less common. They happen only about once every 5 to 10 years. During these earthquakes, people can see seismic waves move the ground. The waves toss objects into the air. Buildings fall down. Big cracks form in the ground.

After an earthquake is over, the ground often shakes again. The new shaking is called an aftershock. Aftershocks are smaller earthquakes. A large earthquake can have many aftershocks.

More than 600 aftershocks happened after the 1995 earthquake in Japan. Many people were homeless because the earthquake destroyed their houses.

An earthquake caused rocks and soil to slide downhill onto this road. What are sliding rocks and soil called?

CHAPTER 4
WHAT HAPPENS NEXT?

In an earthquake, seismic waves make the soil vibrate. Sometimes the soil and rocks on the sides of a mountain shake loose. They tumble and slide downhill. The sliding soil and rock is called a landslide. Roads are often buried by landslides after an earthquake. If houses are on the mountainside, the soil and rocks can bury them too.

In 2001, an earthquake shook the country of El Salvador, in Central America. It caused this landslide. The landslide buried about 300 homes.

Sometimes earthquakes happen near bodies of water. When the ground shakes, the water moves. It mixes in between the tiny pieces of sand or soil. If you stepped on this watery ground, you might sink into it. Sometimes buildings sink into the ground when the soil under them becomes watery!

Some earthquakes happen below the ocean. They can cause a special kind of wave. The wave is called a tsunami (soo-NAH-mee).

An earthquake caused the soil beneath these apartment buildings to become watery and soft. The buildings tilted and sank partway into the ground.

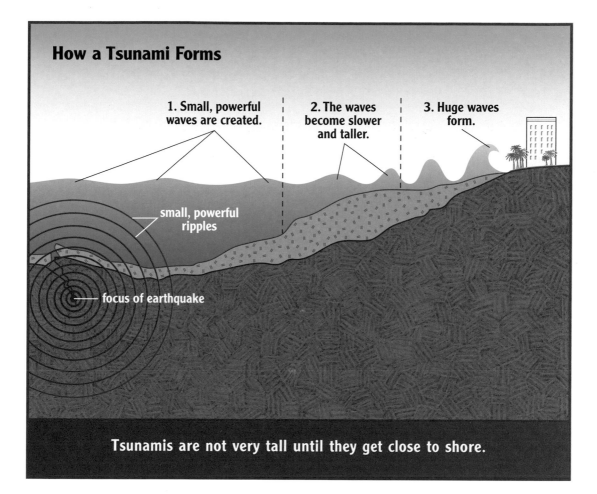

How a Tsunami Forms

1. Small, powerful waves are created.

2. The waves become slower and taller.

3. Huge waves form.

small, powerful ripples

focus of earthquake

Tsunamis are not very tall until they get close to shore.

A tsunami races across the ocean surface. It can travel almost 500 miles per hour. A tsunami is not very tall when it is far out at sea. But it gets bigger as it gets closer to shore. By the time a tsunami reaches land, it can be 50 to 100 feet tall!

In December 2004, a huge earthquake happened beneath the Indian Ocean. It was one of the strongest quakes in history. The earthquake started tsunamis.

The tsunamis caught these people by surprise in Thailand.

People ran when they saw the tsunamis. But many could not get away fast enough to escape the danger.

The tsunamis spread quickly across the ocean. They hit the countries of Thailand, Sri Lanka, India, and Indonesia. Some waves hit eastern Africa. People did not expect the tsunamis. They did not know to go to higher ground. Many people died.

Earthquakes are a danger for millions of people in San Francisco. What can people do to stay safe in earthquakes?

CHAPTER 5
BE PREPARED

Many people live and work in areas where earthquakes happen. People might live there because the weather is nice. Maybe the ground is good for growing food. Fortunately, people can do things to keep themselves safer in an earthquake.

Power lines and buildings can fall down during earthquakes.

First, go to the safest place possible. If you are outside, move away from buildings. Stay away from electric power lines. Don't go near objects that could fall and hurt you. If you are in a car, stop the car in a safe place. Stay in the car until the quake is over.

If you are inside a building, stand in a doorway. Doorways don't fall down as easily as ceilings or walls. If a doorway is not nearby, hide under a big table or desk. It can protect you from falling objects. Stay away from windows and large mirrors. They may break. Never go into an elevator during an earthquake. If the electricity goes out, an elevator may stop between floors.

Children in the Philippines have earthquake drills. They practice taking cover under their desks.

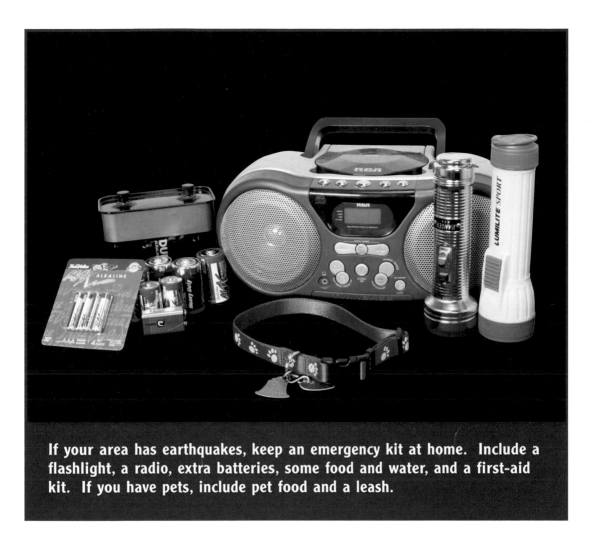

If your area has earthquakes, keep an emergency kit at home. Include a flashlight, a radio, extra batteries, some food and water, and a first-aid kit. If you have pets, include pet food and a leash.

When the shaking stops, go outside. Some damage may be hard to see at first. The building might still be dangerous. Don't go back inside until an adult makes sure the building is safe.

Buildings can be made so that they are less likely to fall down in an earthquake. Tall buildings can be built with materials that let them swing back and forth. This lets the buildings move without breaking. An earthquake, then, cannot easily break apart the building.

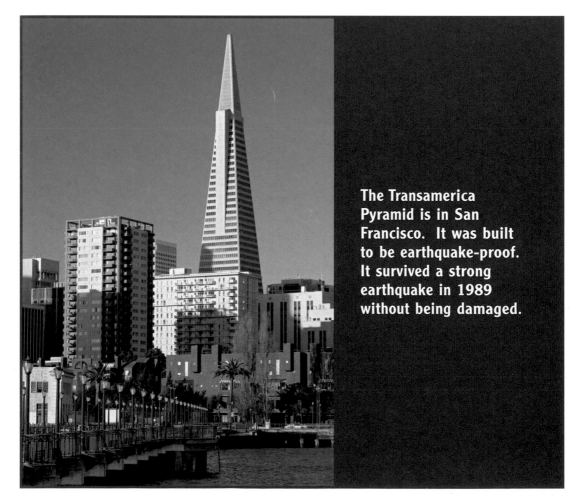

The Transamerica Pyramid is in San Francisco. It was built to be earthquake-proof. It survived a strong earthquake in 1989 without being damaged.

This house in El Salvador will be safe in earthquakes. The walls are made of sticks. Then they are covered by a thin layer of cement.

In some countries where earthquakes happen, people build their homes with bricks made of mud. Mud bricks break apart in an earthquake. Falling bricks can hurt people. But mud homes can be built safely too. People can make the walls out of sticks, long grasses, and leaves. Then they can spread a thin layer of mud or cement on top. In an earthquake, the mud crumbles into little pieces. It doesn't hurt people when it falls.

No one knows when an earthquake will happen. That's why seismologists study earthquakes. They hope to find clues that will tell them when and where an earthquake will take place. They want to be able to warn people ahead of time. Then people would have a chance to go to a safe place or leave the area.

These seismologists are studying a fault. Learning more about faults helps scientists to understand earthquakes better.

Earthquakes have helped to shape these mountains in Yosemite National Park in California. Earth's surface is always changing because of the movement of Earth's plates and earthquakes.

Millions of earthquakes have happened on Earth. People cannot prevent earthquakes. Until seismologists learn more, the best way people can be safe during an earthquake is to be ready for one.

ON SHARING A BOOK

When you share a book with a child, you show that reading is important. To get the most out of the experience, read in a comfortable, quiet place. Turn off the television and limit other distractions, such as telephone calls. Be prepared to start slowly. Take turns reading parts of this book. Stop occasionally and discuss what you're reading. Talk about the photographs. If the child begins to lose interest, stop reading. When you pick up the book again, revisit the parts you have already read.

BE A VOCABULARY DETECTIVE

The word list on page 5 contains words that are important in understanding the topic of this book. Be word detectives and search for the words as you read the book together. Talk about what the words mean and how they are used in the sentence. Do any of these words have more than one meaning? You will find the words defined in a glossary on page 46.

WHAT ABOUT QUESTIONS?

Use questions to make sure the child understands the information in this book. Here are some suggestions:

> What did this paragraph tell us? What does this picture show? What do you think we'll learn about next? What do we call the big slabs of rock that cover Earth's surface? What does a fault have to do with an earthquake? What can people do to stay safer in an earthquake? What is your favorite part of the book? Why?

If the child has questions, don't hesitate to respond with questions of your own, such as: What do *you* think? Why? What is it that you don't know? If the child can't remember certain facts, turn to the index.

INTRODUCING THE INDEX

The index helps readers find information without searching through the whole book. Turn to the index on page 48. Choose an entry such as *seismograph* and ask the child to find out how scientists use seismographs. Repeat with as many entries as you like. Ask the child to point out the differences between an index and a glossary. (The index helps readers find information, while the glossary tells readers what words mean.)

LEARN MORE ABOUT
EARTHQUAKES

BOOKS

Drohan, Michele Ingber. *Earthquakes.* New York: PowerKids Press, 1999.

Harkins, Susan, and William Harkins. *Earthquake in Loma Prieta, California, 1989.* Hockessin, DE: Mitchell Lane, 2006.

Morris, Ann. *Tsunami: Helping Each Other.* Minneapolis: Millbrook Press, 2006.

Storad, Conrad J. *Earth's Crust.* Minneapolis: Lerner Publications Company, 2007.

WEBSITES

FEMA for Kids: Earthquakes
http://www.fema.gov/kids/quake.htm
This website includes stories, games, and activities to help you learn about earthquakes. It also has information about keeping your home and pets safe from disasters.

National Geographic Kids Magazine: Earthquake!
http://www.nationalgeographic.com/ngkids/0403
Learn more about preparing for earthquakes, and watch a video of earthquake damage in San Francisco.

USGS Earthquake Hazards Program: Earthquakes for Kids
http://earthquake.usgs.gov/4kids
Check out earthquake facts, photos, maps, history, activities, and more! You can even send a question to a U.S. Geological Survey scientist.

GLOSSARY

aftershock: a small earthquake that happens after a larger quake ends

crust: the outside layer of Earth

energy: the power to make something move

fault (FAWLT): a crack in Earth's plates where rock has moved during an earthquake

focus: the underground starting point of an earthquake

forces: pushes and pulls

magnitude (MAG-nih-tood): how strong an earthquake is

mantle: the layer of Earth that lies beneath the crust

plates: thick slabs of rock that cover Earth's surface

Richter (RIHK-ter) scale: a number scale used to describe how strong an earthquake is

seismic (SIZE-mihk) waves: waves of energy made during an earthquake

seismograph (SIZE-muh-graf): an instrument that measures earthquakes

seismologists (size-MAH-luh-jists): scientists who study earthquakes

tsunami (soo-NAH-mee): a large water wave made by an earthquake

vibrate (VEYE-brate): to shake

INDEX

Pages listed in **bold** type refer to photographs.